There is, in Kimberly Reyes's *Bloodletting*, an impressive command of diction that, coupled with her precision for clarity, wit and intense observation, produces a poetry of great insight and intellectual alacrity that makes her a brilliant observer of the complexities of the American present. Whether writing about Taylor Swift, the crisis of global warming, or her father, her capacious sensibility allows for vulnerability, humor and the luminous red of bold cultural commentary. Her poems are beautiful studies in form and sentiment. Reyes's poems have managed the enviable quality of being wholly contemporary and present and at the same time unfettered by time.
—Kwame Dawes, author of *Sturge Town*

In *Bloodletting* Kimberly Reyes strips herself bare and asks the same of her readers. "Discomfort is no longer a season," she writes, and in that discernment, we are given permission to not only feel, but allow rage to boil over and set us free. Reyes's poems are so precise, the blade of a knife, carving out the hidden uglies of this world. Full of pop culture references, and the language of the living, this collection dares us to texture everything until we finally find its true center: "I have no idea what to live for if not love," we read & poof this collection becomes an act of deep knowing, purposeful, in a world burning too hot for of our comfort.
—Yesenia Montilla, author of *The Pink Box* and *Muse Found in a Colonized Body*

The unfolding honesty of *Bloodletting*, its cut, just deep enough, feels like a record of a present that might break us. Reyes answers the gaslighting of an entire society with a poet's truth, as she mourns her and our illusions.
—Roque Raquel Salas Rivera, author of *antes que isla es volcán/ before island is volcano* and *lo terciario/ the tertiary.*

Previously Published Poetry

vanishing point., Omnidawn Publishing, 2023.

Running to Stand Still, Omnidawn Publishing, 2019.

Bloodletting

Cover art Archers, Ernst Ludwig Kirchner, oil on canvas,
195 × 130 cm, 1935–1937. Public domain.
back cover art: Erzählende Milli, Ernst Ludwig Kirchner,
chalk on paper, 44 x 34 cm, 1909. Public domain.
Cover design by Shanna Compton
Cover typeface: Avance Pro

Interior design by Kimberly Reyes and Laura Joakimson
Interior typeface: Garamond Premier Pro

Library of Congress Cataloging-in-Publication Data

Names: Reyes, Kimberly, 1977- author.
Title: Bloodletting / Kimberly Reyes.
Description: Oakland, California : Omnidawn Publishing, 2025. | Summary:
"This is a collection of poems about how we find and cultivate love amid
wars, including wars that often go ignored. Throughout Bloodletting,
Kimberly Reyes considers how we define love and who gets to experience
it, paying special attention to the ways that race and sex influence how
we are perceived and valued by society. Through the voice of a Black
woman coming to terms with her own perspectives on
relationship-building, Reyes shows the damage that contemporary culture
can do to women, and Black women in particular. Resisting passivity,
Reyes's poetry cuts through pervasive doom scrolling, virtue signaling,
and parasocial relationships, inviting readers to remember what care is
really supposed to feel like"-- Provided by publisher.

Identifiers: LCCN 2024055849 | ISBN 9781632431660 (trade paperback)
Subjects: LCGFT: Poetry.
Classification: LCC PS3618.E9386 B56 2025 | DDC 811/.6--dc23/eng/20241125
LC record available at https://lccn.loc.gov/2024055849

Published by Omnidawn Publishing, Oakland, California
www.omnidawn.com
10 9 8 7 6 5 4 3 2 1

Bloodletting

Kimberly Reyes

OMNIDAWN PUBLISHING
OAKLAND, CALIFORNIA
2025

Contents

there's a crack in the mirror
and a bloodstain (above) my bed
—*"Bloodletting"*
Concrete Blonde

Red

On a drive through the blanched
straw & mocha Midwest,

approaching neon numbers that could be the price of diesel
or the sum of faded lotto tickets—

I keep seeing her lips,
her lipstick is so red,

on lips that don't ever seem to chafe or crack.
Alexei Navalny—red obstruction's orator—died last night

he could have been dead for months
he survived a poisoning once,

a nerve agent added to his tea,
I wonder if his lips knew before his gut,

waiting in white Tomsk, what his obstruction would cost.
The nerve agent, Novichock, probably made Alexei's

siren blue eyes fade to a pinpoint pupil black
while his pink lungs flooded with blood-tinged fluid

as red as her lipstick—a fire-engine-Radio-Flyer-
Americana-taste-the-summer red,

& it's all we can talk about:
The currency between those red lips,

& if her new man will propose, & what our
bombshell billionaire means for girl power

cause conversations about the Congo, out!
Ethiopia, Yemen, Sudan... beyond passe, &

more horrifically, cancellable! Imagine getting in
the muck, inside out frayed & rudded—Navalny,

once a racist, self-immolated seeing corruption's face
& she's never been more popular! Cool regal red. She won!

Katy who? A fever dream. Beyonce's now a fan
& none of them are gonna give lip

service to Gaza. Shhhhhh—   it's almost over...
& at the Grammy's our girl, leaving red

lipstick on all her champagne glasses, announces
her next album: The Tortured Poets Department (!)

I drive in silence letting the motion of violence lull
me into the necessary numb of pretending that torture

can be contained, colored, appropriated, & appraised—
a different kind of toxin, & a red lip—

I was reading about neighboring Yellowstone,
how it's tens of thousands of years overdue
for a good scream. I know moving back to the coasts
won't save me,
when she erupts,
I'm stuck in this middle-
American hellhole,   so I lean in.
Compartmentalizing magma, mantle, molt,
it can't be healthy.
The shit's been building for millennium

—lean in.

Fratricide

An unforgiving winter is coming   but discomfort
is no longer a season,   manmade extinctions
are the new norm --- ---- ---- ----   that's a different poem...

According to beekeepers, this winter is going to be a real drag
            'em out event   because bees

are already throwing out the excess,   like months early.
 I'm referring to honeybees   & the somewhat unserious

drones are men

& the bees that do the dirty work   of keeping the hive
efficient   are called workers.

These bees only ditch the drones early when they need
to,   not for sport.

Workers are happy to keep the drones around
for as long as it's feasible

            as drones are family: offspring,
partners,

dependents,   & housemates   & relationships
are complicated.

(I've never met a woman who would disembowel
to make a moot point).

When the honeybees know it's going to be especially cold
they pack all their honey in the brood box
for the surviving girl-gang   & their queen.

The *brood box*—as if they know   they are poets.
They stay warm through winter by shivering.

           This silent synchronized

contraction,   this tremble,   becomes muscle memory

(not an overproduced concert of crickets, or the melodrama
of cicadas who leave so much carcass   in their wake)

which keeps the hive a near-human 95 degrees—

       as if our incessant buzzing
       caused these matriarchs to mimic us—

a solemn sentence for those who survive.

Something about spinning like a girl
in a fancy new dress and having a bright
new city all to ourselves
and the chill of for the first time wanting
to say *I need you*
and knowing for the first time
I had something
to lose...
—*my memories of Taylor Swift's "Holy Ground"*

Had we made it past the heat,

the honey,
we could have thawed semi-sweet

& ekphrastic, waking to rewatch
our black & white film,

retracing lines of dialogue
as we stumble

over cryonic sieves
of affection

in a quell we'd call history,
cold fidelity,

as we'd learn new ways
to hate & hard-swallow,

embalming the savor
of when we were present—

an oiled kernel,
a muscle pre-spasm—

forever technicolor

claiming to know the tense in which love happens

is preposterous once you've been there. It's almost as silly
as someone asking "when did you know," or "have you said
it
to each other yet," or "how long have you been together,"
or, better yet, "how long were you together?"
As if answers to any of those questions can reveal anything
but answers about the person asking.

Because of course   the closest thing to the truth
feels like it is always happening and it is still
happening,
and had happened before you met.

And sometimes you just think love is *liking* someone. Like really liking
someone enough to want to be around them for no reason,
when nothing is happening, when nothing is being said, but you feel
like life is finally happening, even if you are just catching their jawline
and no one else knows why you almost dropped your wine.
Like this is maybe why you are alive? To sit and watch them smile
at a sunset BBQ or look up after turning the last page of a book.
That moment of stillness. That hush—an exquisite extrication
when you're unaware of any other earthly vibration.

Then also, at its best, love is petty and smelly. It's pheromones
and the rush of Listerine meeting metal-scarred gums
and mousse and cum-stained jeans and missed classes
and Watchamacallit bars and sweaty palms and always always always
proving what we may be/what we may be still proving
to our 7th grade bullies about being chosen in that way.

But really, you know if someone is/has been in love by how hesitant
they are to kill a ladybug or if they flinch watching anyone

or anything being hurt, even on screen, in a TikTok video,
even if the video is about an ugly moth,
even if the pain is just secondhand, like at a reading, god
at a *way* too long poetry reading, because love, however fleeting,
is a tapping into a new timeline. It doesn't always last,
and we don't all even know that it's happened,
when it's happening,
which is the cruelest of all time thefts.

...shoot another shot, try to stop the feeling
(I wanna) say it's just the way (I am)

(I wanna)

stop the world.... just to stop
the feeling

—maybe *Good Luck, Babe!*
Chappell Roan

(as told to the narrator, to herself)

How to disassociate

You drop the armor
low enough to let a man
pierce fortified muscle

then suddenly it's over—
you see the world as familiar,
walking, throbbing veins
& realize,
people have been performing
coronary bypass surgery,
driving yellow busses of embryos,
flying engorged planes
of families
buckling for more time
together on land

after enduring the pain
that was making soup
of your spine,   & you

hate
a little less.

You'd learned,
you'd surely scab—
get more chances
for someone to hold your hand
during takeoff.

But as years passed &
happenstance unmasked,
grace became the one muscle
resigned to atrophy.

My love for things is partial

After Diane Seuss

I think, because he was only ever partly here.

I like to think of him as fully in his body,
there, as a child, in Coney Island,

happy
eating pee-water franks and vandalizing gray fire hydrants to unleash

cold fury as the black summer concrete and his bare white feet met
relief.

All of his senses were fully working there,
then, before,

as he'd end his day at the window,
waiting patiently for his father to come home.

He was his dad's favorite, he never told me that, his still-jealous
siblings off-handedly make jokes about this, decades later,

long after their father was buried. But then,
my father could see himself in someone else every day,

he could see that his beloved vestige saw himself in him too,
that he truly belonged to someone without needing to beg, buy,

or perfect his way into that sanctuary.
Then, he never worried about the tense of that love changing.

Then, one evening, as my father sat in their first-floor apartment,
he saw death.

He might have seen (we can't be sure 'cause memory betrays
and takes so many parts of the part of him that's here)

his father crossing the street as a man in a feral car unleashed a fury
that would reverberate for decades, on Bayview Avenue.

My father probably saw the life he most cherished leave the earth,
then, leaving him here to spend the rest of his life looking

for the same tenseless recognition, that he likely felt,
he'd never again find.

He was probably eight, or ten.
The age changes each time he tells the story, now,

even though timelines should be easy to verify.
But so many elders have gone on, and so many who were there,

then, also left parts of themselves to the concrete.
I can't imagine that pain,

watching your heart leave its body,
from outside your body

but I do envy the belonging
he's still mourning,

because I think it means there was a time
he was whole.

The water in blood evaporates until there's just red crust.

Bloodletting

...and then Bono said something about the horror of losing beautiful
Israeli children:

"as the sun is rising in the desert sky, Stars of David, they took
your life, but they could not take your pride"†

and nothing about the beautiful Palestinian children who are also
and always dying   and that was enough
to decimate what was left of my resilience.
Bono, the Taurus man I've loved
like a father, second only to my IRL Taurus father.

I'd never been mad at Bono and I've spent 68% of my life angry
with my dad

because he's real

      (us Tauruses are known as being *the most* loyal.)

      but I'm breaking up with all my heroes.

      I don't even talk to my brother anymore

that's a story I can't fully conceptualize
in this timeline.

Months later Bono said it was bewildering to see what the children
of Abraham were doing
to each other,

it was the first time I heard him acknowledge that Palestinians had
human children—

he noted we were witnessing the suffering of Palestinians
after we witnessed the stones thrown at Israelis
as if that was the order of events.   As if that was the history
of Abraham and Goliath.

I'm not big into the bible and family lore. I don't talk to my brother
anymore   and

AND, after well over a decade, I'm renouncing my Swiftiehood.

I took ALL the heat for being a Black Swiftie but then:

Matt Healy (allegedly had TS down bad—allegedly
mocks Black women for sport) —

Ice Spice (a Black woman Healy mocked who TS immediately,
publicly befriended) —

TRAVIS KELCE... Christ!

After the first kerfuffle with Black social media I expected the Queen
of Scheming to know

her new beau dropped his *blaccent* to be   with her,
had previously only dated Black   -BROWN skin
women,

          WASTED the last one's

                    —her name is Kayla

time for five years—which athletes rarely do,

cause they've got practice and diets and it just makes sense
to 'commit'

                                                    whether faithful
                                                    or not,

to the girl on their 'gram

                    she gets the ring,
                    she gets "wifed."

                    Kayla made it to the 'gram
                    but Travis made Kayla a bridesmaid for half
                    a decade, wondering her worth
                    while he got picnic invites and sowed
                    his Midwest oats only to leave her
                    a now infamous

                    X

                    another "single Black female."

She was so close to land—
                            brow barely breaching before
                            reading online comments:
                                "he UPgraded
he Upgraded,
                    HE FINAAALLLLYYYYY UPGRADED."

Kayla very publicly started therapy   after the breakup
and read a poem virtually:

"Dear Black girl, *...You'll hope the ones closest will protect you,*
but you will quickly find out that people don't protect what they don't value.
They'll say you're too much, ...And in the same breath,
tell you that you are not enough."

It goes on:

"They'll say you deserve the backlash and embarrassment
because of your Blackness. You should have known better...
But **Black girl,** *please remember...*
Your value is deep within your heart."

And on:

"The rage of the world is loud..."

Kayla probably loved him.

But you can't trust a jungle fever dude,

You should have known better

fetishization ain't cute,
I learned
that lesson a long time ago. They "slum," they gorge...
and soon their palettes ossify
            their compasses set for the social capitol—
            he was always going home.

            I'm sick of the term "trigger" but my pores scream
            every time I walk by a newsstand with T&T's
            headshots.

Tay should have known/girl powered/reasoned

should have stuck up for Kayla when Travis didn't

                                        —Travis didn't
                                        after all those years, public
                                        videos of him and her
                                        and their familiars—

'cause Tay does
'discarded X,'
'one that got away,'
'You should have known better,'

for a living,
done it a billion times.

                        But it's not about that capital.

Tay hurt me   because I thought we were   like *girls,*
could be girls,   cause she got me.
It didn't matter that just the idea of her could enter spaces

I couldn't

that she's always been white, well off, blonde,
charismatic, thin—   I still loved her for documenting (?)
incessant pain   'cause earnest heartbreak was my story
and she wrote it so well.   She cosplayed as a sympathetic character

the character was all that mattered

and how was "Mean" not a banger?

Something about *words like*
swords and *knives—*
being forced off your feet
again
by the merciless

then
there was something about the bully
yelling over a football game
with nobody listening...

I mean, I was,
          listening

                    cause she got *me*
                    (almost like she was a misfit Black girl!)

way more than other bullied oddities,   who looked more like me
more than her **foil** Kanye   (let's keep it honest amongst us,
Kanye didn't care about Black women before he very obviously
did not care about Black women)

but I'd still never get the invite to Tay's cookout, her chocolate chip
cookie and white girl wine parties, be a part of her
Victoria's Secret/Cover Girl/femme fatale white woman army

because I'm not a white woman. I don't know why I can't
let this reality sink in: my womanhood can not be loud
and erring
unlike the white woman I know IRL
who pretend to be woke
only to proudly post their all-white woman wedding parties and white
woman engagements
despite their POC "allyship" and DEI commitments
(yes, these were my "friends"
but,   growing up my NYC looked like *Friends* NYC
so I'm not sure I ever had a chance),

I was always the only Black girl in my "friend's" pics on the 'gram.

You should have known better

They'll say you deserve the backlash and embarrassment

How was Kayla supposed to know five years of entry
into a mostly Black male club,   would still not grant
her ~~equal~~ access to the club?

                    We could maybe interview Shannon Sharpe

                    a Black man football guy

                    one of many maybe Travis was trying to impress

                    with his fine Black girl girlfriend

                    but it was an ironic miscalculation—

                    Shannon served an all-teeth

                    on-camera testimony

                    saying that Travis 'upgraded'

                    with the Swiftness

                    The thing is if a man goes out of his way
            to put women   that don't look like the women
            that cleared the most treacherous swells to rear him
            on a pedestal,   if he is branding himself
            with the quiet part: he doesn't want his children
            to look like his mother or his sisters, if he can't stand
            his reflection,   we aren't talking
            about preference,   we're talking about
            someone trying to phase himself out of existence
            while taking us with him.

Maybe only we can hear his earth-

shattering pleas.

We see.

Shannon later brought Amanda Seales into Club Shay Shay

but he couldn't handle her *too muchness:*
she was the right type of "bright"
(he juked and jived about her capital, "your mom is white?")
and the wrong type of bright
for his audience—

Amanda wore a keffiyeh

and felt entitled to interrupt an ignorant man
who couldn't understand why she wouldn't
fall in line

why she wasn't wearing a ring...

she was wearing a keffiyeh

and went inside The Club
to talk community and family

as Katt Williams had blown the Club doors open
for 'Truthtellers' in 2024

but there was no mention of Palestine
and not of the intertwined in Sudan, The DRC, Haiti...

       weeks later 'Uncle Katt' taped a live special
       made a joke about enslaved women
          his ancestors
       single handedly ending slavery

       by *seducing* their captors

        their rapists
        their torturers
        his ancestors

the crowd, Black and white, erupted.

You'll hope the ones closest will protect you,
but you will quickly find out that people don't protect what they don't value.

My brother and I would watch Amanda's streams together

and bond over how ~~smart~~ Black women are constantly

being played in our faces

by a certain type of man, showing their whole ass

because we are the women

who remind them

how vulnerable

we are

You should have known better.

Bono made his rant over "Pride (In the Name of Love),"
my first favorite song. He decided to piss on the plight
of 2.3 million Palestinians living in apartheid Gaza
on a $2.3 billion, NY basketball-funded, Vegas arena
while repurposing a song about Dr. Martin Luther King Jr.
If this wasn't the universe on a soapbox about false idols...

But TS never pretended
to be anything other than the queen of all white woman
at least? Never needed to go off-brand,
not even for her white chocolate man.

She maybe reneged about not being *cheer captain*
and being *on the bleachers*...

did a 180 in fact, on the biggest stage,
and invited her token light skin Black friend
(see also Ice Spice, poem pg. 2)
to the Superbowl
as sidekick and shotgun.

Tay, Lively and new friends   with Kayla's former besties
so very drunk and Blonde and blithe—ending their shiva for Lilith
people, I now realize,
have been telling stories in "we"s as opposed
to "I"s   (liking and unliking racists and MAGA posts)
since high school

that's not my story.

Here's the thing

Red saved my life.

I'd just broken up with the one person I'd arguably loved

but I can't tell that story with any perspective, either,

because I didn't grow up conditioned to recognize

and distinguish

contempt from

fascination from

adoration from

fetishization from

care

fast enough.

Yes, I'm triggered.

But maybe I knew something was off,

with Bono and me,

when he was willing to perform
without his best friend since high school

the only man,
he said,

that could ever really make him mad

and still recover—
(again, we are Taurus)

the man that has become his brother

and I bought tickets   anyway   to have pics on the 'gram

to a U2 show   without Larry
          the heart, the beat, the drummer
unraveling the U2 that's always been U2   to gain capital

so perhaps,

perpetually,

my hand was on the trigger.

But back to Tay's new man

'cause that's how this works now. My brain becomes TikTok scroll
and,
preposterously,
dating injustices
everyday femicides

        "the rage of the world is loud"

parallel genocide

              of course not
              obviously not

              but

pain is personal and runs parallel   and relative
and

I have no idea what to live for if not love.

Actually forget Tay's dude.
I hope Kayla can.

I'm so sick of trying to fight empire
at home, in bed.

I went home and remembered why I lost

my only sibling: because he was happy to ~~downgrade &~~
erase us to be in the proximity of white mediocrity.
He'd exclusively dated Black women all his life...I heard
I'd never met them, he never brought them around,
but I saw a few pictures online.

(The algorithm anticipated.)

His girlfriends progressively got lighter.
He got bolder.
Then he *Ye'd.**

Got lost in the most questionable, white-presenting
white-identifying (!?) Puerto Rican
with a ~~predatory~~ *preference* for Black men

—she clocked and claimed the pedestal—

they exchanged rings, illiteracies

(listen: there was talk of Fox News
and "all-sidesing" at her address
before I dissociated—
I *had* to amputate the limb)

gave her everything he'd previously withheld
from the women
who looked like the women
whose scarred, arched backs
he leapfrogged
on his way
to the Capitol.

He chose violence,

casual warfare,
firing up all manner of ballistics:
indifference, carcass, cruelty...

splicing through familiar   flesh
exposing our collective upbringing
                    pulling
                         a reverse draw, Joker of avarice.

Meanwhile

I watched my parents'
preset blinders go up
for what they must have seen
as their last chance for ~~a wedding~~

their **one** idea of respectability.

I'm trying to have some loyalty. That should stay in this family.
I should attempt performance

                         even if I'm just

suffocating our echoes.

The rage of one person can be cataclysmic.

*Please also see Kanye's tragic trajectory,
particularly his dating life.
It would appear that his protests about injustice,
that often bleed as misogynoir,
are more about his inability to access
the patriarchy
than actual justice.

He's not alone.

(...also see TS's song "The Man")

† From an early U2 show at the Las Vegas Sphere to us fans, and the world.

no one wants to be vulnerable
when there is a pacification war.
vulnerability, like poetry,
is a promise
—Roque Raquel Salas Rivera

**It is maybe time to admit that Caitlin Clark
only thought about/had to think about herself
in her final NCAA game,
and will never be
the GOAT**

After Hanif Abdurraqib & Claudia Rankine

Angel Reese has nearly perfect baby hair

ends curved with the precision of Artemis' bow,
yet soft and doe-like as an Oread's touch,

much to the chagrin of

some white women behind screens &
some Black men in bowties
on tv, who say that this Angel

got what no one heard her ask for:
to be the Villain

because babygirlhood
is not reserved

for girls who look like an Angel
from Baltimore

it's exhausted
intrinsic law
for girls who look like a Caitlin
from Iowa

to play & publicly learn

& taunt & publicly lose
without opening the skies
& triggering the seasons

but Angel stayed cool,
as the rains came

& the cameras panned to Caitlin
singing "Lovestory" at warmups.

These playoffs were advertised with videos of little blonde girls
cheering for a Caitlin—
            and I wonder what the babies
            were learning to revere.

All they saw on the screen was a white woman in a sea of mostly Black
women &
            crowd thunder & joy eruptions
            as the ball went in

                                    for the skin team.

I've gone to school & worked with & loved women who have this
imprinting.

            They don't even have to be white (or women).

            It's an almost perfect system.

I grew up   watching Magic smile for the cameras,

all teeth

                           Midwest white

on cue for the lights

like a Cheshire cat in the night,

while Larry got to brood
with vain
moods   and a crankiness
that would come more natural to me.

It's diabolical that they've written rules,
and continuously ask us

to play ball.

Dancer and Audience by Ernst Ludwig Kirchner

The Male Gaze/Mating Game That is Compartmentalization

Object

        Object

Object

        Object

(person I care about)   Object   Exotic object

     Insecure object   Drunk object

     (person I know)   Shiny   Object

        (person I should care about)
     Object   Object
  (person I could care about)

     3am object   Reluctant Object Familiar Object

(inconvenient person)   Object Object Dull Object

        Person to care about

(for now)

Sleeping Nilly by Ernst Ludwig Kirchner

You don't need to cheat,

just compete against a Black

woman, it's baked in.

—November 5th, 2024

The name I was called by is already lost.
Its face orbits around me
like the sounds of water at night,
of waters falling into waters.
And the last thing to go is its smile,
instead of my memory.

—Alejandra Pizarnik

Misogynoir begins at home

My mom is the only other Black woman I interact with,
on a daily basis, since
as long as I can remember.

Her nickname for me

as I progressed into puberty:

the letter S

for the shape of my body.

I recoiled, perhaps embodying the namesake, at this homemade
shame.

Who was I/who was she insisting I be...

Siren

Segment

Shrewd

Spinster

Shrew

Sinister

Supernatural

Sorrowful

Sorry?

The Sigil

After Lucy Grealy

I sometimes forget how grateful I should be to have a face.

At nine I was obsessed with my playground's swings:
rubbered black padding covered
hot gray asphalt beneath all but one
whose absence   I hadn't noticed
as I ran to fly—arms extended, legs splayed—
through the extra three feet
into the sky
my daydreams promised.

On a forceful downswing,
my eager weight shifted,   unbalanced,   as my torso slid
off the warm metal,
face meeting hot bare concrete—   nose, cheeks, and chin
as buffer.   I didn't feel the floor until my mother came
running—
eyes as darting black alarm.

There was no pain— only new, bare wetness   where skin was.

That evening there was whispering between parents:
scarring and *social implications* that didn't permeate,
as if grade-school me
wasn't yet me.   I remember we had blood red spaghetti,
and I don't think it was my lack of vanity that freed me from tantrum
and fear so much as residual obedience to the stop signs
in my mother's face, a hint of tryptophan in the tomatoes,
and how I was still trying to stick the landing.

I don't know how my face came back unscathed—
the asphalt had every right to keep its integrity—

but I eventually reclaimed the vestige

that now awakens my phone,
the sigil that, when letting the nightmares win,
I've sometimes allowed
men to swipe left or right on,

the face that brightens my mother's eyes,
especially at airports, after long spells
of her only looking at its representation,
maybe thinking of all the respectable degrees
and symbols I've amassed,

a comfort that keeps the knots from forming in her womb,
keeps the stop signs from returning
at the thought of losing me,
to men, to The State,

the picture she'd have to show The World,
The Media—if necessary—to have it decide

if I should live, if I should be honored in power if I die
...it's the face I try to ignore most mornings,

because I cannot handle
the wholeness of it.

The algorithm is insolent.

My Face ID pretends to not know me

...facial recognition software... algorithms were significantly more likely to mix up black women's faces than those of white women, or black or white men.

One factor could be that it is "harder to take a good picture of a person with dark skin than it is for a white person..."

—WIRED

The system I was using worked well on my lighter-skinned friend's face, but when it came to detecting my face, it didn't do so well, until I put on a white mask...

—Joy Buolamwini, computer scientist and digital activist speaking about her MIT Media Lab project: The Coded Gaze

it isn't altogether unclear
what the glass is reflecting back

the rind padding around my eyes
the extra weight on my cheeks

the scowl beginning to crease my face
the Midwest heat grease

my newly acquired rust color
my maladaptive lack
of vitamin D

the flyover dead spots forming
the way this land marks me.

It is not unclear
who the glass is reflecting back

        I thought it was retinal fog it clocked
but it's more about patterns and projections...

the dead spots

                                    in photos   my phone stores

assessing me   exhausting

reminders I can't turn off

friends & lovers & siblings,   even animals who are "memories"

the notifications are

                    shameless

as if my phone also wants to belong
to someone who takes more ~~presentable~~ indelible molds.

A Heartbeat in a Cemetery in Tennessee

It's been over a year (I think)   I'm here for a writers'
conference & one of the teachers reminded me how trees talk
to each other underground.   I think of their tap roots
braiding the earth into place as a local man enters me
& I get that much needed hit, the rush
of forgetting why cemeteries have become rare places of comfort.

The sassafras branches converge as lattice for the moon
that's climbing through leaves
to laugh at the awkward humping   & out-of-rhythm sighing
happening between the headstones. But the intoxicating madness
of cicadas,
who are also out banging their backs against trees in a guttural plea
for sensation
/ annihilation, drowns out the sounds of our incongruence.

We are not planting roots tonight, just laying the peat.

Now I remember it's only been six months, 'cause God plants
selective amnesia & that's how memory is supposed to work
without the throughline of afterglow, as all of my
muddy faces rush back from the soil.

"I contend that there's a very special excellence that comes from being forced to create an entire culture, an entire ethnicity, an entire existence of being Black American, without even being able to attach to the land you're on, which means your body has to be the soil—

Our body has had to be the soil...

...Because divide and conquer isn't simply just about keeping us apart as cultures,

divide and conquer isn't simply about keeping us apart as people in the same community,

baby, divide and conquer is also about keeping you
apart from your soul."

—Amanda Seales
"What Would the Ancestors Say??"

Aerial root

... in brief, there is nothing so indigenous, so completely 'made in America' as we."—W.E.B. Du Bois

I don't know the difference between being home and being home-grown, but I don't think anyone does.

I also don't understand indigeneity but, of course, I of all people wouldn't. (I think that means home.)

Yet the idea my home wouldn't be the smell of Coneflower, Lobelia, Woodland Iris, and Red Twig Dogwood is toxic ignorance. Cotton Palms, Zebra Plants, and String of Beads may have felt like a home stolen

to distant elders, but I never knew those people.
I do know my mother

always kept a Sansevieria in the house and has always given me its babies when I start over somewhere new. The Snake Plant was given to her by an elder who got it from an elder my mom calls *grandma* (our most prized and tangible elder). Grandma's Snake Plant and its babies have travelled from South Carolina to NYC to Chicago to Paris to San Francisco to Cork to Lincoln. I'm not good at keeping plants alive but grandma's plant is indestructible. The Sansevieria has roots native to Africa

and we of course don't know how it got to its first home in South Carolina

but it's renowned for its air purification qualities.

This is my home
this thin edge of
barbwire.

But the skin of the earth is seamless.

—Gloria Anzaldúa

The Buzz

After Mayra Santos-Febres

"Low-frequency noise annoyance has been reported worldwide over
several decades—so much so, there is now a global hum map
and database"

The Omagh hum: what is the source of the town's mystery moan?
—The Guardian

We don't know when the noises were first detected.

          But we know that low frequency grazings have been
heard around the world for decades: Taos, Auckland,
Frankfurt, Detroit, Omagh. aaa

                                        agH
                                        aaaaagh.
                                        You're
                                        all very
                                        grating.

There's speculation that it could be your submarines, windfarms,
UFOs or just your 5G rattling the earth to annoyance. Ce. Ceea.
Ceeeee. See

more people live beneath the earth, and under the sea, than above—

the catacombs of Rome and Paris with tunnels of reburied

at discos way above 432
                            hertz
it all does   in mazes, mausoleums...

as the ones
who jumped
ship
      before crossing
        The Atlantic's   music—   —a brined soup
of

brown noise séance
                & potluck

                waiting

for the last round of children to return

that's what we,   listen(ing) to.
        you are

No one sprouted out of any ground.
We're all just a bunch of fish who slithered out of water
and eventually crossed land bridges, were kidnapped, sold,
ran, or rode our way to new seedlings

the most adaptive went underground
for a while.

...All the dreams that we were building
We never fulfilled them
could be(en) better, should be(en) better...

All the homes that we were building
We never live'd in
Could be better, should (have [be]en) better...

If we lose the time before us
(Maybe the) future will ignore us

Yeah
Lessons in love

—*"Lessons in Love"*
Level 42

Calling me everything but a child of God.
But they can't do nothing else
'cause they ain't got what they wanted yet.

—*Ma Rainey*
From August Wilson's Ma Rainey's Black Bottom

Ghosting

21st century romance is phantastic & felled
in ways our ancestors might envy, save the barbaric spells

at their disposal. When I look up & around my family tree
& see how the ~~necropolitics~~
           barter
             promise

          corrosion
                  of partnership has barely shifted—

I'm not sure how to define agency, or if it was my choice to opt out
of the karmic ties of intimacy: so many brown gnarled

knuckles & stalled branches intervened, so much must surrender
to the soil.

I'm aberration who has learned to become aberration.

It's my go-to move when I zero in on an object of disaffection
      & their indifference to my humanity   begins to eclipse

          my incapacitation.

      But once the darkness shifts
the spell breaks,

         I'm controlled, complete

   &,

limb by limb,
    pixel by pixel,   begin to fade out of

    every   future they could   ever
      envision draining me in.   _____

      I'm   no longer   there
    like
  my moms,   patchwork scarf on head,

      inflamed
with worry,

still smiling,
    soothing the baby.

I'm   no longer   there

lighting the candles   they forgot to buy

as we celebrated,

our eldest holding her breath

     as she remembers the fight over burnt bacon &

blows,

     trying not to cry.

I   disappear   without

before they notice,

I   was only

                   ever
                            parts

anyway.

From a distance I can see   the rug
      rerouting the room,

                  catching their ankles first,

pulling their timelines from underneath,

      & it's cavity sweet
      indulging my Gemini moon

        as I short circuit the   dopamine

interpose the self-assured wet dreams

        blocking their

     sweaty-thumbed texts

           refusals of defeat—

Never asked for war...

Cursed my vestige
For ages
Faced the world like a ghost
Hunted the night
Streams of invisible smoke
Obeying my elders
To pass on alone

Tried to hold on to you...

But here comes more combat

As cruelty is the point

& all of my (heartbreaks)
Started off (kin)...

So I'm ready for combat.

—*A retelling of Taylor Swift's "The Archer"*

Notes

Turns out this book is the end of a trilogy. It's astonishing how much poetry gives and takes without us even knowing, but this is indeed the end of a story.

It was risky to write such a topical poem, especially as the centerpiece of a collection, but this book asked me to be raw and to strip down any pretense of what was masking what was igniting my slowly churning rage, so that's what I attempted to do.

I was the biggest TS fan when it was very *not cool* to be a Swiftie (remember when Kim and Kanye were winning? TS had a pretty wicked Saturn return) and it was just us forever teens, actual teens, and parents at her concerts. Then a mirror broke. It has nothing to do with her (sigil). I don't know her. But the music is a part of my history.

I loved creating the following, layered playlist for your supplementary convenience, and will do my best to keep it active but please know that this list and its lyrics were always meant to be injected via written word.

I was a music journalist in a past life for a reason. Peel the onions and read (listen) between the lines.

Bloodletting Soundtrack (although perhaps not always in this order)

Bloodletting by Concrete Blonde
Red by Taylor Swift (as subtext)
Brother and Sister by Erasure (as subtext)
Holy Ground by Taylor Swift
Mine by Taylor Swift (as subtext)
Pitch the Baby by Cocteau Twins (as subtext)
Passion by Rod Stewart (as subtext [for the book])
Mad About You by Sting (as subtext)
What Is Love? by Howard Jones (as subtext [for the book])
The Last Day of Our Acquaintance by Sinead O'Connor
Joey by Concrete Blonde (as subtext)
Pride In The Name of Love by U2
Mean by Taylor Swift
You Belong With Me by Taylor Swift
Thieves Like Us by New Order (as subtext)
Bad Blood by Taylor Swift (as subtext)
Look What You Made Me Do by Taylor Swift
The Man by Taylor Swift
Love Story by Taylor Swift
Round & Round by New Order (as subtext)
(going underground by the jam)

-

Lessons in Love by Level 42
Good Luck, Babe! by Chappell Roan
This Corrosion by The Sisters of Mercy
Who Needs Love Like That by Erasure (as subtext)
Humpty Dumpty by Aimee Mann (as subtext)

The Archer by Taylor Swift

YouTube Bloodletting Playlist

Apple Music Bloodletting Playlist

Artistic Acknowledgements

I was really hesitant (and late! in the process) to submit these poems and, for many reasons, some of them never left this book, so I'm especially grateful to the journals that took in what were essentially parts of one massive poem.

"claiming to know the tense in which love happens" won the 2024 Love and Eros Prize, thank you to *Palette Poetry* and John Lee Clark.

"Fratricide" and "The Buzz" were published by *The Offing.*

"The Sigil" and "Had we made it past the heat" were published by *Banshee.*

"It is maybe time to admit that Caitlin Clark only thought about/had to think about herself in her final NCAA game, and will never be the GOAT" and "I grew up" were published in the *Killens Review of Arts & Letters*

"The Male Gaze/Mating Game That is Compartmentalization" and "My Face ID pretends not to know me" were published in *Obsidian: Literature & Arts in the African Diaspora 51.1.*

"Ghosting" first appeared in the *North American Review.*

An earlier version of "Aerial root" was published online with the Nebraska Writers Collective.

The quotes and/or allusions to various artists' lyrics, or real or imagined people, are considered "fair use."

All of the artwork is by Ernst Ludwig Kirchner, including the cover image, *Archers*, and the back image, *Milli*, and they are all in the public domain.

Personal Acknowledgements

Thanks to Ken Price, Kwame Dawes, and Marco Abel for their academic knowledge, grace, and advice.

And Ken, as a first-generation* eldest daughter in always predominantly white settings, and a Capricorn rising (!), I've always felt like a rocket whose flesh was burning through the atmosphere—as my ambition propelled me forward without any cover. Mentorship was the armor I'd always yearned for, and I'm (becoming) so much softer for having a prolonged taste of it.

Thank you to Luis Othoniel Rosa for teaching a Latin American poetry class in Nebraska and for unapologetically teaching Black Puerto Rican poets.

Thank you to Michele Wilson, Alicia Smith, and Kayla Fink for being my mental health team in Nebraska cause, my god, did I need that!

Many thanks to Emma Loughney and our often interrupted yet storied 2am pub talks for the clarity of "The Male Gaze/Mating Game That is Compartmentalization" sonnet.

Many thanks to Yesenia Montilla and her CantoMundo workshop for inspiring "My love for things is partial."

Thank you to CantoMundo and my fellow CantoMundistas. Nebraska is cold, so it's necessary to have a place to warm up and regenerate.

Thank you to every artist whose work I've quoted for inspiration. Yep, every one.

---

* and by that I mean first-generation college graduate. Please don't get me started on how long my ancestors have been here, and how much they've contributed to making "America Great" for everyone but themselves.

Thanks as always to Omnidawn. This was a deeply personal book that didn't have much outside editing so thank you for taking a chance on it. Many thanks to Rusty and Laura for their careful read(s).

I can't mention you all so Up The Rebel County and everyone there who consistently supports me, I'm so honored to be a wee blow in (what like) every year.

Everyone else, cause I consistently go overboard, IYKYK.

Archer at Wildboden by Ernst Ludwig Kirchner

Bogenschütze by Ernst Ludwig Kirchner

Kimberly Reyes (Aries Venus & Mars) is a poet, essayist, teacher, pop culture scholar, 2nd generation NYer, and the author of three full-length poetry collections. Kimberly has received fellowships, scholarships, and/or prizes from the Poetry Foundation, the Fulbright Program, the Academy of American Poets, CantoMundo, and many other places. Her work has been published in various outlets including *The Atlantic*, *The Village Voice*, *Poetry Review*, and *american poets*.

Bloodletting
by Kimberly Reyes

Cover art Archers, Ernst Ludwig Kirchner, oil on canvas,
195 × 130 cm, 1935–1937. Public domain.
back cover art: Erzählende Milli, Ernst Ludwig Kirchner,
chalk on paper, 44 x 34 cm, 1909. Public domain.
Cover design by Shanna Compton
Cover typeface: Avance Pro

Interior design by Kimberly Reyes and Laura Joakimson
Interior typeface: Garamond Premier Pro
Interior design by Kimberly Reyes and Laura Joakimson
Interior typeface: Garamond Premier Pro

Printed in the United States
by Books International, Dulles, Virginia
Acid Free Archival Quality Recycled Paper

Publication of this book was made possible in part by gifts from
Katherine & John Gravendyk in honor of Hillary Gravendyk,
Francesca Bell, Mary Mackey, and The New Place Fund

Omnidawn Publishing Oakland, California
Staff and Volunteers, Spring 2025
Rusty Morrison & Laura Joakimson, co-publishers
Rob Hendricks, poetry & fiction editor,
& post-pub marketing
Jeffrey Kingman, copy editor
Sharon Zetter, poetry editor & book designer
Anthony Cody, poetry editor
Liza Flum, poetry editor
Rayna Carey, poetry editor
Sophia Carr, production editor
Elizabeth Aeschliman, fiction & poetry editor
Jennifer Metsker, marketing assistant
Avantika Chitturi, marketing assistant
Angela Liu, marketing assistant